BANNACK
CRADLE OF MONTANA

TEXT AND PHOTOGRAPHY BY F. LEE GRAVES

MONTANA MAGAZINE
AMERICAN & WORLD GEOGRAPHIC PUBLISHING
HELENA, MONTANA

DEDICATED

TO THE SOB'S, AS THEY CALL THEMSELVES— MEMBERS OF THE ORGANIZED SONS (AND DAUGHTERS) OF BANNACK WHO FEEL THAT BANNACK HAS A UNIQUE STORY TO TELL AND ARE VERY WILLING AND DEDICATED TO HAVING IT TOLD.

ISBN 1-56037-003-3

Text © 1991 F. Lee Graves
© 1991 American & World
  Geographic Publishing,
  all rights reserved
P.O. Box 5630, Helena, MT
  59604
(406) 443-2842

William A. Cordingley,
  Chairman
Rick Graetz, President & CEO
Mark O. Thompson, Director
  of Publications
Barbara Fifer, Production
  Editor

Design by Linda Collins
Printed in Hong Kong

INTRODUCTION

One of the problems of writing a book about Bannack is that there is quite a lot of information, much of it conflicting. It is evident that a few of the previous authors on the subject have even tended to add their own versions and comments, historical fish stories if you will. There usually is the thread of truth in the story, but sometimes the particulars are obscure. In this book, I have attempted to ferret out the facts, and have added phrases like "local legend states" to indicate conflicting stories or to color the story with a different version. For example, the location of the gallows and graves of Plummer and associates, the location of the Ives-Carrhart gunfight, the killing of Chief Snag, and histories of some of the Road Agents (and even a complete list of Road Agents) have conflicting accounts.

I have stayed away from sources that are largely undocumented or differ greatly (even sometimes heretically) from most reputable historians. Fact bashing, Vigilante bashing, and establishment bashing seem to be popular themes of "history" right now, and I have stayed away from those biased views, too.

Although there are many people, too numerous to mention, to thank for help with this book, I wish to thank several people and organizations who contributed both advice and support: my sister Karen Gordon who chauffered me around to several historical sites pertaining to the area and kept the sense of humor piqued; Oren Sassman of Salmon, Idaho for his encouragement and for the use of his invaluable master's thesis of 1941 entitled *Metal Mining In Historic Beaverhead;* David Walter and the Montana Historical Society, and Sonja Williams and the Beaverhead County Museum; and my wife, Carol, for generous comments and criticism. Most of all I would like to thank Dr. Dale Tash, professor of history at Western Montana College of Dillon, and park manager at Bannack. Dr. Tash gave me invaluable assistance, information, and complete access to the "Bannack Archives." Without his advice and encouragement, this book would have been a much more difficult project.

> *Bannack, the cradle of our state,*
> *is a quaint little place,*
> *that lives only in the history she has made...*
>
> Professor Thomas J. Dimsdale
> *The Vigilantes of Montana*

CONTENTS

Above: Tranquility before sunset enhances Grasshopper Creek, with Bannack Peak in the background.
Left: Giant paintbrush (Castilleja miniata).
Facing page: Bachelor's Row.
Front cover: Meade Hotel and Skinner's Saloon. TOM DIETRICH PHOTO
Back cover: The changing face of Bannack. Top: A 1900 view looking northwest across dredge ponds, the dredge Fielding L. Graves *visible in left background.* (PHOTO COURTESY OF THE AUTHOR)
Bottom: Bannack State Park in the 1980s.
Title page: Detail from one of Bannack's two jails.

Lee Graves was born in 1946, the son of Fielding H. Graves and Viola Graves of Dillon. Lee's father, and his grandfather Harry Graves, were born at Bannack, where his great-grandparents arrived in the early 1860s. The author's father, a banker, was also a writer and historian, so Lee grew up with stories of Henry Plummer and the Vigilantes and Road Agents. An employee of the state of Montana for nearly 20 years, he also has served on the Board of Directors of Custer Battlefield Historical and Museum Association. He is Past Grand Historian for the Masons of Montana, and has published numerous historical articles and landscape photographs. Lee and his wife, Carol, live in Helena.

BANNACK STATE PARK

FREIGHT TRAIL TO VIRGINIA CITY

Water diversion ditches

FREIGHT TRAIL TO CORINNE, UTAH

1. FRENCH HOUSE—This was the residence of George French, who built the coffin of Henry Plummer. He also ran the Bannack Brewery west of the house, where the parking lot is now located. That structure was remodeled in 1985 and is the visitor center.

2. RESIDENCE—Chandler and Lelah Stallings lived here from about 1935 until they moved to Dillon in 1965.

3. TURNER HOUSE—Spokane Mining Company offices. The building used for Art Contway's Post Office, residence, and barber shop about 1918.

4. DRUGSTORE AND ASSAY OFFICE—Reported to be the A. J. Oliver express office, and was one of the original structures at Bannack. Early photographs show it being used as a drugstore and assay office.

5. DOCTOR'S OFFICES, RESIDENCE, AND STORE—Built in 1880, this building housed doctor's offices, a school and stores. The location is supposedly where the Territorial Council Building (Senate) met.

6. MEADE HOTEL—Built in 1875-1876 at a cost of $14,000 as the Beaverhead County Courthouse. After county seat moved to Dillon in 1882, remodeled as the Meade Hotel, with an extensive addition to the rear. Served as a hotel until the 1930s.

7. JACKSON HOUSE—Owned by the Jacksons, proprietors of the Goodrich Hotel. Also served as a post office.

8. SKINNER'S SALOON—Originally built in the fall of 1862 by Cyrus Skinner on Yankee Flat, this saloon was moved to its present location by 1863 and was reputed to have been the "headquarters" of the Road Agents.

9. BACHELOR ROW CABINS

10. GRAVES HOUSE—Built in 1867 by carpenter William Roe, one of the first frame houses in Montana. Acquired by Fielding L. Graves, for whom the house is named.

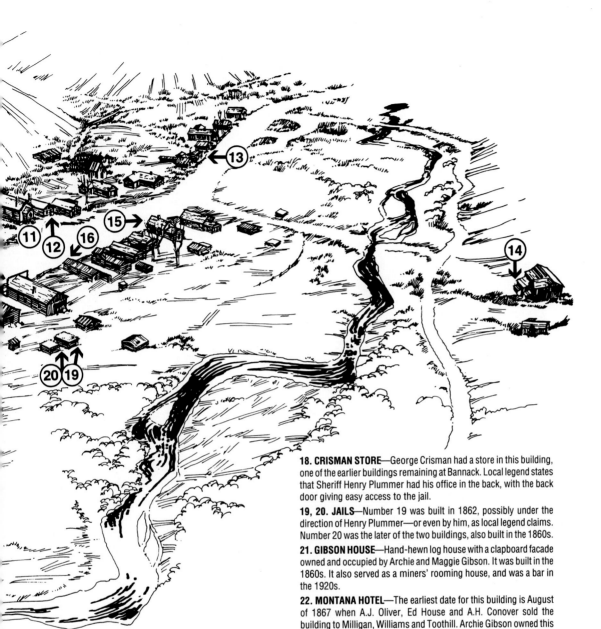

11. CHURCH—Built in 1877 under the direction of Methodist missionary William Van Orsdel. Used as a school building in the early 1920s.

12. RESIDENCE—Legend has it was the Methodist parsonage.

13. XAVIER RENOIS HOUSE—One of the oldest cabins in Bannack, said to have been built by French Canadian Xavier Renois in 1862.

14. MILL—Bannack Mining and Milling Mill was constructed in 1917 at a cost of $235,000. Chandler Wellington (Chan) Stallings was superintendent of construction. Also called the Graeter, Hendricks, Apex or Bannack Mill.

15. AMEDE BESSETTE HOUSE—One of Bannack's founders, "Medde" lived here until his death in 1919. Leo Musburger, Bannack teacher from 1931 until 1933, lived on the back east side and paid rent of $10 per month to the I.B. mining company.

16. APEX MINING COMPANY HEADQUARTERS—Built in the late 1920s.

17. CASEY HOUSE—In the early 1870s, E. M. Brown ran the Brown and Co. Bakery and Saloon here. It became the Gauthier Boarding House, and then Mary and Joe Rebish had a cafe here in the 1920s. Mabel Ovitt lived in the back of this building until her death in 1968, and maintained a rock shop/second hand store in the front part.

18. CRISMAN STORE—George Crisman had a store in this building, one of the earlier buildings remaining at Bannack. Local legend states that Sheriff Henry Plummer had his office in the back, with the back door giving easy access to the jail.

19, 20. JAILS—Number 19 was built in 1862, possibly under the direction of Henry Plummer—or even by him, as local legend claims. Number 20 was the later of the two buildings, also built in the 1860s.

21. GIBSON HOUSE—Hand-hewn log house with a clapboard facade owned and occupied by Archie and Maggie Gibson. It was built in the 1860s. It also served as a miners' rooming house, and was a bar in the 1920s.

22. MONTANA HOTEL—The earliest date for this building is August of 1867 when A.J. Oliver, Ed House and A.H. Conover sold the building to Milligan, Williams and Toothill. Archie Gibson owned this building and ran a rooming house for many years. School was held in the building in the 1940s.

23. MASONIC LODGE AND SCHOOL—Built in Greek Revival style in 1874. The first Masonic Temple in Montana and one of the first school buildings still in existence.

24. CARRHART HOUSE—George Carrhart, Road Agent friend of Henry Plummer and George Ives, lived here until his death in Skinner's Saloon in 1863.

25. RYBURN RESIDENCE—Built about 1896. Dr. Robert Ryburn, early Bannack physician, lived here until he moved his practice to Dillon in the 1920s. The house was occupied by various families until the 1960s.

26. GRAETER HOUSE—Initially the residence of Augustus F. Graeter, for whom one of the gold dredges was named. The ell on the right was added by Tom Underwood in 1934, along with the fireplace. He also installed Bannack's first indoor plumbing here. Underwood used the building in back as a blacksmith shop.

27. RESIDENCE—Built in 1886. Rufe and Montana Nay Mathews lived here beginning in 1886 and raised their family here. In August of 1954, Georgie and Bertie Mathews gave the house to the Beaverhead County Museum for the Bannack State Park Project.

28. THE GOVERNOR'S MANSION—Built of the logs from Governor Edgerton's home, which burned in the mid-1920s. Chan Stallings built the existing structure in the 1930s.

CLIMATE

Visitors to Bannack naturally experience all kinds of weather, and Bannack is in a land of extremes. Instead of the temperate weather of Dillon and the Beaverhead Valley, Bannack is more like Wisdom and the Big Hole Valley, which frequently hold the wintertime daily record for the coldest spot in the 48 contiguous states. In the summer, however, one is sure that the expression "dry and dusty" originated there. Bannack personnel of the Montana Department of Fish, Wildlife and Parks often are asked, "Why did man choose such an inhospitable place for Montana's first capital?" The truth of the matter is, man did not choose this tucked-away corner of the Grasshopper Valley, the valley instead chose man by offering a very rich deposit of gold to those who dared brave the hardships to get there and find it. Once there, only a few got rich; most did not. Of those people who came to Bannack, each one got something, maybe something he was not looking for. This book will tell the stories of Bannack, and of some fascinating people who contributed to her history.

Above: Hoar frost on sagebrush paints a cold picture over Bannack's landscape. The first building is the Apex Mining Company office.
Left: Looking north from Bannack Peak across town toward 10,568-foot Mt. Baldy. The Bannack-Virginia City Road heads north up Hangman's Gulch in the center.

In the Grasshopper Valley.

BEAVERHEAD GEOLOGY

Earth has always been an extremely restless planet, and taking a look at the variations of geological types and formations found in Montana shows that clearly. Montana's geology began a thousand million years ago when sand, muds and limy oozes were laid down, layer upon layer. Time eventually hardened the deposits into formations of shale, sandstone and limestone several miles thick. About 60 million years ago, the mountains of western Montana were formed by incredibly massive shifts of earth. Enormous explosions beneath the earth forced lava to extrude onto the surface. The strata of western Montana were crumpled, thrust, and pushed around, resulting in a rough overlay of mountains, valleys and plains. Geological fine tuning began taking place with rains, winds and other storms stroking the land, sometimes not so gently, and sculpting the beautiful formations we see today in such local mountain ranges as the Pioneer, Beaverhead, Tobacco Root and Blacktail, and such valleys as the Beaverhead, Big Hole, Horse Prairie and Centennial. Rivers and creeks formed, not only having their geological effect on the land, but also adding immense beauty. Later on, it would be primarily around these bodies of water that man would settle, for creeks

and rivers provided not only the necessary water for life, but also a source of animals, fish and birds for food, roots and berries for nurture, and willows and trees for shelter.

During the period of the Rockies' formation, minerals such as gold and other precious metal were deposited in formations known as veins and drifts. They were oftentimes buried hundreds of feet deep, as well as laid on or near the surface of the ground. Most of the gold lay buried, covered by dirt, rocks and other debris, and it took the action of creek and river to expose the precious metal. One might say it was just lying there waiting to be discovered. The Indians might locate some of the ore, but generally found it useless since it was too soft to be fashioned into tools or arrowheads. Lust for the precious metal did not come to this valley until many years later.

EARLY MAN

Archaeological evidence found in the Beaverhead County area and near Bannack indicates that man has inhabited southwestern Montana for several thousand years. Early prehistoric man gathered in clans and hunted in groups. Men of the clan hunted, and fashioned tools out of whatever material suited their needs, while the clan women gathered berries, roots and other edibles.

Prehistoric man used hunting weapons such as the atlatl, a device to extend the throwing arm and hurl a spear with more killing power than a man can. Artifacts found in southwestern Montana include the Folsom Point, which dates from about 10,000 BC, the Milnesand Point from 8,000 BC, and more recent points such as the Agate Basin, Meserve, Angostura, McKean, as well as a proliferation of other artifacts from about 500 AD to 150 years ago.

Scrapers, knives, awls and fleshers often have been found in conjunction with the

various points. In one site near Bannack, primarily large fleshers or hand axes have been found, but few if any points, and nothing made from the very common obsidian. Most of the artifacts are made from hard rocks that are easy to flake, such as the "volcanic glass" called obsidian, which came from either the Obsidian Cliff area of today's Yellowstone National Park or the obsidian quarries in the Centennial Valley. Other native rocks utilized were gneiss, chert, flint or agate.

Early man is also evidenced in the area by tipi rings, at least two "medicine wheels," a few wickiups made of lodgepole pine, and buffalo jumps. Tipi rings are quite common in Beaverhead County, and are usually located near creeks or streams. The tipi ring is a ring of rocks, usually about 16 feet in diameter, set on the sides of the buffalo-hide tipi to hold it in place, especially during high winds. When the owner decided to move on, the rocks, usually about a foot in diameter, were rolled off the hide and left on the spot.

Several lodgepole pine wickiups are also found in the area, although they are quite rare. As with most camps, they stood near water, but one was in a stand of lodgepole, undoubtedly for concealment. The wickiups are usually about six feet in diameter and about seven feet high inside. Their exact purpose is unknown, but modern theories favor the idea that the Tukudika Shoshone, a subgroup of the Lemhis, built the Bannack-area wickiups and used them as fairly permanent shelters. One such site, south of Bannack State Park, has been investigated extensively. It consists of a wickiup in a large cave, a rare example since most of these wickiups were built in stands of timber.

Medicine wheels have been identified near Bannack, such as the one southeast near Clark Canyon Dam. Much speculation has occurred as to the purpose of the large stone "wheels," a purpose shrouded in the mists of time. Theories range from religious rites to determining the equi-

noxes and full moons. The Crow Indians say that the medicine wheel was given them by the Great Spirit to show how to build a tipi.

Early hunters created numerous pish-kuns, or buffalo jumps, in the Bannack area. Beginning in the days before they had horses, native people stampeded buffalo herds over steep drops, then quickly dispatched injured animals below. A general skinning "party" then took place. Following on-site processing, some meat was used immediately, with most being made into pemmican and dried for future use. These sites, of course, yield numerous buffalo bones as well as numbers of artifacts such as arrowheads, knives and fleshers.

Top: Tipi rings dot western Montana and are obvious reminders of early Native Americans who lived in the area. Fourteen tipi rings comprise this camp, each about 16 feet in diameter. Above: Fairly common in Beaverhead County, lodgepole pine wickiups are usually found in stands of timber. This wickiup was inhabited by the Tukudika Shoshone and is about 200 years old.

EARLY DAYS AT "BANNIK"

This story was related in the January 7, 1890 Dillon *Tribune* by James Harby, early Bannack resident:

"Pilgrims were arriving daily at the new Eldorado, lank of stomach and lean of purse. The mails came regularly to the camp, each letter with Uncle Sam's levy of green stamps properly affixed, yet the Postmaster with a commendable enterprise assessed a further tax of $1.50 upon each letter received. It was a paying office. We give the following experience of a friend at that time in his own language.

'I arrived late in the evening with a dyspeptic-looking mule train, a lank and hungry pilgrim with $1.35 cents in my pocket which was not enough to buy a square meal, although I did not know it. I had written home before leaving Alder Gulch to have them forward me a remittance to Bannack.

'...My first act upon entering camp, therefore, was to hasten to the log hut that served as a post office. Yes, there was a letter for me; also a pair of gold scales handy. Upon receipt of "twelve bits" in coin or dust I could have the missive. He would not even allow me to see the superscription. It was only by long and earnest entreaty that he consented to give it to me in return for my little all. He did so finally, however. I tore the envelope open and read as follows:

Deer friend Jim: I heer from yure
foaks that you have went to Bannik. Deer Jim,
I have a faver to ask. Will you staike me out a
good clame there for me? I will cum out in
the spring, if you can sell my clame for a gode
pile, do it and send me the munny.
          Yures trooly. Jake Henderson.

'You can imagine my disgust at learning the contents of this valuable letter for which I had paid my last ten cent! The kindhearted postmaster, however, though he had hesitated to deliver the letter to me loaned me a couple of ounces of dust until my money should come'."

THE COMING OF THE WHITES

In 1803, President Thomas Jefferson purchased the Louisiana Territory from Napoleon of France for $15 million. This territory comprised what is now much of the northwestern United States, including about four fifths of today's state of Montana. Jefferson wasted no time in setting up an expedition to explore his newly acquired land, and organized the Corps of Discovery. Its leader was 28-year-old Meriwether Lewis, President Jefferson's private secretary. Lewis selected as co-captain his friend William Clark, an expert geographer and cartographer who knew frontier life and Indians well. On May 14, 1804, the expedition left St. Louis, Missouri on the journey that was to take two years and four months.

The first white men to come into today's Beaverhead County undoubtedly were members of the Lewis and Clark Expedition. Captain Lewis recorded the event of passing by the mouth of Rattlesnake Creek on August 14, 1805: "As the early part of the day was cold, and the men stiff and sore from the fatigues of yesterday: we did not set out until seven o'clock. At the distance of a mile we passed a bold stream on the right, which comes from a snowy mountain to the north, and at its entrance is four yards wide, and three feet in depth: we call it Track Creek." The snowy mountain recorded by the expedition is the 10,568-foot Mt. Baldy. The next day, with a small group moving ahead of the main expedition, Captain Clark passed by Grasshopper Creek and recorded, "About a mile further [from what is now Barrett's Station] is a second point of rocks, and an island, about a mile beyond which is a creek on the right, ten yards wide and three feet three inches in depth, with a strong current: we called it Willard's Creek after one of our men, Alexander Willard." Two

days later, Lewis's and the main party reunited near Clark's Canyon. Later on that same day, August 17, Sacajawea was reunited with her tribe, the Shoshones, and her brother Cameahwait, their chief, whom she had not seen since her capture by the Minnetarees many years before. The group reached the Pacific Coast that year, and spent the winter of 1805-1806 at their "Fort Clatsop" near Astoria, Oregon.

On the return trip, the expedition split up on July 3, 1806 at Traveler's Rest near Missoula, with plans to meet on the Yellowstone River. Captain Lewis took nine men and went down the Bitterroot River, ultimately northeastward to the Great Falls of the Missouri. Captain Clark took 20 men over what is now Gibbons Pass to a "Boiling Spring" that is at Jackson. From Boiling Spring they traveled southeast and eventually down Willard's Creek (Grasshopper Creek) on July 8 and through the site of future Bannack. Captain Clark recorded, "Tuesday, 8, we crossed the valley along the southwest side of Willard's Creek for twelve miles, when it entered the mountains, and then turning S."

The next white man to visit the Bannack area was undoubtedly a fur trapper 20 or 30 years after Lewis and Clark, who possibly set a few traps on the banks of Grasshopper Creek to take a share of the plentiful beaver. Willard's Creek was just another small, insignificant beaver stream somewhere in the Rocky Mountains. (Beaver still swim in the creek today. A good place to watch for them is behind the jail.)

GOLD

The first recorded discovery of gold in Montana occurred well north of here in 1852. François Findlay, better known as Benetsee, found a small amount of gold in the gravel he panned at Gold Creek, one of the headwater streams of the Columbia River. The gold was of such an insignificant amount that he did not consider it worthwhile to develop. He told other mountain men of his discovery, but little was done. In the autumn of 1857, James and Granville Stuart prospected at Gold Creek. They found gold in fair quantity, but lacked the proper supplies to obtain much of it. Rumors of gold persisted, and brought a few miners from the played-out fields of California and Idaho.

July 28, 1862 was the date of Montana's

When Sacajawea, who was with the Lewis and Clark Expedition, first observed the Point of Rocks on August 8, 1805, she knew she was in the homeland of her people, the Shoshoni. The promontory is located about fifteen miles northeast of Dillon on Highway 41.

NATHANIEL P. LANGFORD

Nathaniel P. Langford was 30 years old in 1862 when he joined the first Fisk Expedition to western gold fields.

N. P. Langford ended up in Bannack, since the Idaho goldfields had played out. On November 12, 1862, a man named William Bell died of mountain fever; his is believed to be the first natural death in the camp. Before Bell died, he requested a Masonic funeral if at all possible. As Acting Master, Langford arranged and carried out the ceremony, the first organized Masonic activity in what became Montana.

In 1863 in Bannack, Langford and others began to organize the first Masonic Lodge for Montana. But by the time the dispensation arrived from Nebraska in June of 1863, most of the Masons had moved on to richer gold fields, mainly Alder Gulch. Nathaniel Langford affiliated with Virginia City #43 (1) and later with Helena #10 (3). In 1866, he was appointed the first Grand Historian of Masons of Montana. Three years later he was elected Grand Master of Masons of Montana and was the fourth in the lineage of Grand Masters.

In 1870, he and his friend Cornelius Hedges became members of the Washburn Expedition, whose purpose was to explore "Colter's Hell," today called Yellowstone National Park. Upon establishment of the park by Congress in 1872, N. P. Langford was made its first superintendent, a position strictly of honor for it was without salary or benefits. He held this position until 1877. In 1872, Langford was appointed bank examiner for "all the Territories and Pacific States." He was an honorary member of the Montana Historical Society and made many valuable historical contributions throughout the years. Perhaps his most significant contribution occurred in 1890 when he published *Vigilante Days and Ways,* one of the standard works on the Vigilantes of Montana. Unfortunately for modern readers, many original Vigilantes were still alive and he respected their wishes "not to tell too much." Nathaniel Langford died in St. Paul, Minnesota in 1911 at the age of 79.

first great gold strike, the Grasshopper Diggings. John White, William Eads, John McGavin and a small party of "Pike's Peakers" (they had pushed north from Colorado) stopped on the banks of Willard's Creek to get some rest and to do some prospecting. A gold pan was soon put into the creek gravel and the elusive gold came forth with such abundance that this discovery led to the greatest rush for the West since the California Gold Rush in 1849. The actual site was below, or east of, Bannack approximately two miles.

By the time winter set in, Bannack had grown to a population of approximately 500 people. It could hardly have been called a town, for there were no permanent buildings yet. For the most part, those people who came to "the diggin's" that first year were boomers, people who would hurry off to the latest strike with no intention of settling, but only to strike it rich. Wickiups, tents, lean-to shelters, tipis, as well as a few hurriedly constructed cabins, greeted new arrivals as they came over the hill on the Salt Lake Road. When rain fell, the streets and sidewalks—which were one and the same anyway—were quagmires. It was not a place that one would write home about, except perhaps in the most colorful of epithets. The winters were worst, with temperatures often settling well below zero for weeks at a time.

Saloons were mainstays of mining camp entertainment, especially in the winter when there was little else to do but drink and gamble. These saloons were poorly heated, drafty, smelly, and certainly did not have the sort of clientele that decent people would associate with. Their adornments were quite simple: perhaps a barber chair, poker tables, benches around the walls, and of course a makeshift bar—often with upright logs for bar stools.

Drinks were so watered down that it is no wonder that most customers drank their whisky "straight." Fighting became a common pastime, and quarreling was a way of life.

...3 was a hard ...ows thawed and ...ed, more miners ...e intent to ...population ...n 3,000 ...her 2,000 ...rasshopper, ...r imagin- ...and once ...was in full ...r claims at ...erwise ...," or taken ...r was ...to see ...chants, who tra... ...ake City, Utah or... ...on head at Fort B... ...er. Prices we... ...ake a nice profi... ...our sold for $... ...-pound sack, sugar at 65¢ a pound, and tea at $2.25 per pound. Whisky, a staple of the mining camp, sold for $4 to $8 per gallon, depending upon quality. A plug of chewing tobacco sold for $7 per pound in gold dust. Considering that an average miner who worked for wages earned about $8 to $10 per day, prices were inflated.

The first formal Thanksgiving dinner in Montana took place at Bannack in 1863, thanks to the generosity of the outlaw sheriff, Henry Plummer. Plummer had been an outlaw for several years, his clandestine career having spanned several states—only in the West, as far as anyone has been able to determine. Part of his plan was to appear as the suave and law-abiding sheriff that he wasn't. Harriet Sanders, wife of Wilbur Fisk Sanders, later described the Thanksgiving feast most eloquently: "Henry Plummer desiring to be on good terms with the Chief Justice, Mr. Edgerton, and my husband, to prevent suspicion arising in their minds that he was engaged in the nefarious occupation of brigandage, with well-timed

display of hospitality, invited Chief Justice Edgerton and wife, my husband and me to dinner on Thanksgiving Day. Considering the meagerness of delicacies in the market and the extortionate prices charged, even for the necessities of life, that repast was one of the most sumptuous dinners I ever attended. Not only was a local market drawn on, but in carrying out his shrewd plans to quiet and evade the suspicion of his neighbors, he sent to Salt Lake City, at a distance of five hundred miles, and everything that money could buy was served, deliciously cooked and with all the style that would characterize a banquet at Sharry's [a prominent New York restaurant of the day]."

Plummer had ordered a turkey from Salt Lake City, which was freighted into Bannack at the total cost of $40.00. Thus the outlaw sheriff was responsible for the first traditional Thanksgiving dinner in the Territory just six weeks before he was hanged by Vigilantes. Yes, prices were high…but life was cheap.

Bannack (c. 1900) looking northwest, showing the dredge ponds of the F.L. Graves. Approximately 400 people lived in Bannack at the peak of the dredging period.

BANNACK SCHOOLS

Many miners who moved to Bannack brought their wives with them, and a few had young families. At first, subscription schools were set up, where parents paid the teacher a set amount periodically, usually weekly. During the winter of 1863-1864, Professor Dimsdale in Virginia City charged two dollars per week for school, and the subscription teachers at Bannack undoubtedly charged a similar fee. One of the first such schools in Montana opened in Bannack in the autumn of 1863 under the direction of Mrs. Henry Zoller in her home. Regular school books were nonexistent in the territory, so books generally were borrowed from anyone fortunate to possess them. The Zoller subscription school lasted about two months.

In October of 1863, the niece of Gov. Sidney Edgerton, Miss Lucia Darling, held school in the Edgerton home at Bannack—the first school in Montana of which there is a definite record. The first term lasted until Christmas, when the holidays and severe cold weather closed school until spring.

Classes at Bannack were held in various homes and locations until 1874, when the school and the Masons built a building together, the classroom occupying the first floor and the Masonic Temple the second. At times, the school had more students than it could handle, such as in the early 1900s when there were about 65 students in grades one through eight. When that happened, the first five grades attended classes in the school building itself, with students of grades six through eight meeting in the church.

School was taught at Bannack until the 1940s, when low population made it impractical to conduct school for so few students. Local children then attended school at Dillon, Jackson, Polaris or Grant.

THE CIVIL WAR

The Civil War (1861-1865) was one of the saddest and bloodiest wars in which America has ever been involved: brother against brother and father against son, fighting on American soil. The West, and in particular Montana, owes much of its settlement and development to the Civil War. Men came west to escape the carnage of battle for many reasons: to start a new life after they lost everything, because they were physically unable to fight, for moral reasons, or personal reasons such as laziness and desertion. The majority of men saw the West as a promised land where one could get a new start and pick up where life left off before the war. Gold discovered at Bannack in 1862, in Alder Gulch at Virginia City the following year and Last Chance Gulch in 1864, was a great enticement to men who had little, if anything, as a result of the War Between the States. Men of all kinds moved to the newly founded gold camps at Bannack, Alder Gulch, Nevada City, Summit, Junction City and Last Chance Gulch. Most came either to "muck and moil for gold" as Robert W. Service, the Bard of the

Yankee Flat, now sporting a patch of cottonwood trees, was located on the southwest side of Bannack. It was abandoned prior to being dredged over about 1900. The Bannack to Salt Lake Road goes up and over the hill to the left of the draw.

Yukon, put it so poetically; a few came to offer goods and services to the miners and prospectors.

Western gold towns were often divided into two camps that reflected the inhabitants' feelings about the Civil War, and Bannack was no exception. Yankee Flat on the southwest side of Grasshopper Creek was where the Yankees or Union sympathizers lived. This suburb of Bannack consisted of about a dozen cabins and a large circular building called the Round House, constructed as protection against Indian raids. The main part of Bannack, where the town primarily is today, was the Confederate part of town. Following the Civil War, Bannack seemed to finally concentrate around the Main Street and to branch out from there. Yankee Flat was dredged over about the turn of the 20th century, and nothing original of that location remains today. Many of the buildings located at Yankee Flat had been moved to the main part of Bannack. Skinner's Saloon, a prime example, was built on Yankee Flat late in 1862 and was moved about February of 1863 (the exact date is unknown), to its present location.

VIGILANTES AND ROAD AGENTS

Each man brought with him beliefs and ethical values that largely dictated his actions and relations with his fellow man. With the good men inevitably came the bad, who leeched from one gold camp to another, robbing and murdering or otherwise plying their personal skills in a selfish and nonproductive way. Men such as Henry Plummer, Buck Stinson, Ned Ray, Cyrus Skinner, Boone Helm, Long John Franck, Bill Bunton and George Ives were quick to move into a virgin gold camp where their true natures were not known. In Bannack, an organization of toughs quickly developed, known as the Road Agents or Innocents (by their password "I am Innocent"). The Road Agents soon had moles, or snitches, in many businesses in the new gold camps of southwestern Montana. They got word of a gold shipment or a stagecoach passenger carrying large sums of money, and promptly relayed the information to gang leaders.

Such wealth seldom reached its destination.

The ringleader of the gang, Henry Plummer, wasted no time in getting himself elected sheriff, in May of 1863. Plummer was even quicker about appointing two of his henchmen, Buck Stinson and Ned Ray, as deputies.

Skinner's Saloon, the hangout for the Road Agents, saw the killing of George Carrhart in 1863, and numerous other shootings. Owner Cyrus Skinner left Bannack late in 1863 and went to Hellgate (Missoula) where he was hanged January 25, 1864 by Vigilantes. In 1869, the building became a mer–cantile and remained so for nearly 60 years.

15

GEORGE CARRHART

Road Agent George Carrhart lived in a small cabin that still stands in Bannack, just west of the Masonic Temple. George's history is unknown, but he probably came from the East, as did most Bannack residents.

In front of that cabin during the winter of 1862-1863, violent disagreement flamed between Carrhart and another Road Agent, George Ives. When a discussion about some forgotten topic developed into a heated argument, both men procured pistols. Ives ran to a nearby saloon, Carrhart grabbed his from inside the cabin, and the two commenced shooting at each other.

Ives barely missed Carrhart, his bullet striking the cabin wall. Carrhart hit Ives in the groin and ended the fight. Reports state that the two soon made up, and that Ives lived with Carrhart the rest of the winter. Lead seldom settles arguments in this manner.

Carrhart met his death in Skinner's Saloon, the hangout for the Road Agents and other roughs, when gambler George Banfield and miner Dick Sapp got into a poker game. Banfield's love of winning overrode his common sense, and he "abstracted" a card from the deck to gain the superior hand. Sapp accused him of cheating and borrowed a pistol from Dr. Bissell. Lead was slung around Skinner's Saloon.

At first the only effect of the impromptu fray seemed the shooting of "Toodles," a small dog. Resting under the poker table, it collected three fatal pistol balls in its body. While lamenting Toodles' demise, the men heard a groan from a bunk along the wall. Upon examination by the good Doctor Bissell, George Carrhart was found shot in the stomach. He died a short time later in extreme agony.

Such was the final chapter in the life of George Carrhart. Reports stated that he was an extremely handsome man, well educated, and that he had even served in the legislature of one of the western states, possibly Nevada. According to his chroniclers, however, his love of whisky and the barroom life was his downfall.

Plummer and his group infiltrated every decent group and endeavor in the mining camps—except the Masons. The Road Agents had watched the Masons with suspicious silence ever since the group of 76 brothers met at William Bell's funeral in November of 1862. It has been reported that Plummer once inquired about Masonic membership. If so, he was quickly discouraged because rumors already had spread about his life of dubious distinction prior to coming to Bannack. Plummer soon became not very well trusted, even if he was the sheriff. So far, no Road Agent has been found to have held Masonic membership.

That the Road Agents had a grip on the area in 1863, few informed persons would have disputed. It was not safe to walk down the main streets of Bannack and Virginia City after dark, and even sometimes in broad daylight. Travel was unsafe because robbery of both stagecoaches and horseback riders was common.

Only three miles north of Bannack on the Bannack-Virginia City Road is a promontory appropriately named Road Agents' Rock. So many robberies took place at that site, that many a stage driver breathed a sigh of relief if he passed the point without getting held up.

The vast majority of people in the camps were hardworking, good people who grew increasingly weary at the growing violence and almost open disdain for law and order. George Ives' robbery and brutal murder of the Dutchman, Nicholas Tiebalt, in December of 1863 near Nevada City appeared to be the straw that broke the camel's back. Ives had killed young Tiebalt for $200 in gold dust and a span of fine mules, and had hidden the mules at a friend's ranch on the Big Hole River. Tiebalt's body soon was discovered, and the trail led to George Ives. The people of Alder Gulch were outraged at the senseless and brutal killing of such a well liked young man and demanded justice. Ives was tried by a miner's court in Nevada City, the prosecutor being Bannack resident Colonel Wilbur Fisk Sanders, who happened to be in Virginia City on business. Adjudged guilty, George Ives was hanged by the neck until dead on December 21, 1863. (The spot of this first Vigilante action is marked today in Nevada City.) Quickly the Vigilantes organized—with a president, treasurer and secretary, and companies headed by captains—and wasted no time in furthering the cause of justice in area communities.

After the Ives execution, the Vigilantes began to investigate further the organization of outlaws they knew to exist. A scouting party of 28 men, called the Deer Lodge Scout, left Virginia City for Deer Lodge for the express purpose of apprehending the comrades of George Ives.

The moon was nearing full, which gave them light to travel at night. The leader of the expedition was Captain James Williams. On the way to Deer Lodge, the party met Red Yeager, unbeknownst to them a member of Plummer's gang.

Yeager had just carried a letter from George Brown, corresponding secretary of Plummer's band, to the Road Agents in Deer Lodge, warning them of the Vigilantes' work by the message, "Get up and dust, and lie low for black ducks." When the Scout arrived at Deer Lodge, they found that the Road Agents had just been warned and had fled. Williams and his weary party decided that they must capture the messenger. They captured Red Yeager in a wickiup a few hundred yards up Rattlesnake Creek from the Rattlesnake Stage Station, and returned to Dempsey's Stage Station, where he was questioned along with George Brown. Finally the Road Agent pair was taken to Lorraine's Ranch at present-day Laurin. The Vigilantes decided not to take Brown and Yeager to Virginia City, since there was the possibility that the two would be liberated by their friends. At 10 P.M. on January 4, 1864, the two Road Agents were awakened and told they were to be hanged. Brown begged for his life, but Yeager was much

more composed, as if resigned to his fate all along.

Red Yeager proceeded to name Henry Plummer as chief of the band, Bill Bunton as a stool pigeon and second in command, Cyrus Skinner as fence, spy and roadster. Among others listed were George Ives and two of Plummer's deputies: Ned Ray as council-room keeper at Bannack, and Buck Stinson, roadster. Red Yeager and George Brown were escorted to the banks of the Passamari (now Ruby) River, where they were hanged from two cottonwood trees. Brown's last recorded words were, "God Almighty, save my soul." Yeager was a little more poetic; after he shook hands with his executioners he stated, "Good-bye boys; God bless you. You are on a good undertaking." (Incidentally, Passamari is a Shoshone word for "stinking water.")

Stories circulated at Bannack about the hangings of Ives, Brown and Yeager. Plummer and his men became nervous, wondering what the Vigilantes knew and what they were going to do about it. Things were "getting hot" for the Road Agents, and many made plans to leave the country. The Vigilantes anticipated such plans, and decided to act quickly. The Alder Gulch Vigilante leaders had met and decided to enlist the aid of the Bannack Vigilantes and hang Plummer, Stinson and Ray. Late in the evening of January 9, 1864, John S. Lott, Harry King and two other Vigilantes from Alder Gulch arrived at Bannack with news from the Virginia

Built of eight- to 10-inch logs, the Bannack jail never saw a jailbreak. Outlaw sheriff Plummer did not spend time in his own jail, but upon capture was taken directly to the gallows.

Top: The Masonic Temple.
Inset: The breadboard square-and-compass emblem.

MASONS AT BANNACK

The Bannack Masonic Temple is the first in Montana and is built on the second floor above one of the early schools in Montana. Although Masons had been active here from the beginning, Bannack Lodge #16, AF&AM (Ancient Free and Accepted Masons), did not receive its charter from the Grand Lodge of Montana until October of 1871. For the next three years the lodge met in a house owned by member Fred Peck. Then the lodge proposed, and the school board accepted, the shared building that visitors see today.

Lodge minutes of May 18, 1874 record that "Bros. Christian Mead, George W. Dart and Fielding L. Graves were appointed building committee and limited to $1200.00 for building hall." Although the exact date is not recorded, it is presumed the Bannack Masons first met in their new temple that autumn.

As on the front of every Masonic Temple, there must be a Square and Compass emblem to announce that the Masons meet there, but the early Bannack Masons were hard put to install the universal emblem on their building. No suitable piece of hardwood for carving could be found in the entire town. Finally, a hickory breadboard that had traveled from a comfortable home in the East was offered by Mrs. Emily Drury Graeter, wife of Beaverhead pioneer miner and active Mason Augustus F. Graeter. James S. Ferster, a Bannack carpenter and Mason who had come to the gold camp in 1863, produced the carving, which still hangs on the front of the Bannack Masonic Temple.

City company and their request for cooperation. Undoubtedly, Wilbur Fisk Sanders was one of the first they contacted. The execution of Henry Plummer, Ned Ray and Buck Stinson was ordered for the next day. During the afternoon of the 10th of January, Road Agents brought three horses into Bannack. The Vigilantes believed Plummer and his deputies planned an escape, so they finalized execution plans.

Immediately before dark, Plummer was making his rounds through town and was returning to Yankee Flat, where he lived with his in-laws, James and Martha Vail, in a cabin next door to the Sanders family. To cross Grasshopper Creek from Bannack to Yankee Flat, one had to cross a footbridge. As Plummer approached the bridge, he met Mrs. Sanders crossing into town. Plummer, the account states, tipped his hat and politely spoke, neither party realizing that at that very moment, Mrs. Sander's husband was planning Plummer's capture and execution for within the hour.

The evening was crisp and clear, with no moon to illuminate a landscape well below zero. The Vigilantes organized into three small companies, each going about its deliberate task of capturing one man before meeting the others near the gallows. The gallows was located about a hundred yards up Hangman's Gulch on Bannack's north side, and had been constructed by Sheriff Plummer himself not a year before, to hang a horse thief named Horan.

One company of Vigilantes, led by William Roe, arrested Buck Stinson at Toland's cabin on Yankee Flat, where he was spending the evening. Ned Ray was captured by Frank Sears and Harry King as he lay passed out on a gambling table at a Yankee Flat saloon.

Henry Plummer was at the Vails' cabin. Martha Vail, his sister-in-law, answered the knock at the door, greeting several Vigilantes led by John S. Lott. Plummer was asked to accompany them, which he

3-7-77

3-7-77. This mysterious combination of numbers has captured the imaginations of students of the Vigilantes and Road Agents ever since the Old Timers who knew its cryptic significance refused to reveal its meaning. But those numbers struck terror into the hearts of Road Agents on whose cabin doors and tent flaps they were tacked. Most took the hint and left the country before they were hanged.

Because no one knows for sure, many theories exist to explain 3-7-77.

The most widely accepted theory today is that the numbers are the dimensions of a grave: 3 feet wide, 7 feet long and 77 inches (6'5") deep. The suspected Road Agent who received such a warning had only so long to get out of town, or he would end up in a grave of those dimensions.

The least plausible theory is that the Vigilantes had hoped to rid the territory of Road Agents by March 7, 1877. But why would the Vigilantes have allowed themselves 14 long years to rid the territory of such an undesirable and dangerous group?

One of the more intriguing theories is that 3, 7 and 77 represented three specific individuals in the Montana Vigilantes. Many, if not most, of the Vigilantes (as well as the Road Agents) had come from the California gold fields and followed discoveries from camp to camp before reaching the Grasshopper Diggings and Alder Gulch. Many of those miners had been members of vigilance committees in California, especially San Francisco—where they referred to themselves only by numbers known to other committee members. It is likely that numbers 3, 7, and 77 were prominent California Vigilantes who later made use of their vigilance committee expertise in Montana.

Another theory along this line is that the numbers originated in Colorado, with the same explanation as California's.

A few people hold to the theory that the numbers represented the vocations of men involved in the first organized activity of the Vigilantes: 3 lawyers, 7 merchants and 77 miners.

Several theories ascribe a Masonic connotation to 3-7-77. Beginning with the premise that Masons formed the first Vigilance Committee in the area, one theory is that the 3 signifies an ancient Masonic quorum.

Another related interpretation is that 3 signified the number present at the first Masonic meeting in Montana Territory, held on Mullan Pass in September of 1862. 7 signified a modern quorum. 77 is the number of the first organized Masonic activity in Montana (the burial of William H. Bell at Bannack on November 13, 1862), with the 77th person being the deceased.

Still another Masonic theory is that the 3-7-77 originated from the Bell funeral, since N. P. Langford, who conducted the service, read from the 77th verse of chapter 37 of Ezekiel.

PLUMMER GALLOWS

The gallows one sees up Hangman's Gulch today is a replica, the original having been on the other (west) side of the gulch and much nearer to town. That original gallows was constructed by Sheriff Henry Plummer in 1863 for the hanging of a horse thief, John Horan. Its next use was the hanging of the three Road Agents on January 10, 1864: Ned Ray, Buck Stinson and Plummer himself. The fifth and last hanging on this gallows was that of R.C. Rawley on October 30, 1864. In the interim, the gallows—about 10 feet tall with a crossbar about 12 feet across, stood as an ominous warning to lawbreakers and malcontents.

In the 1860s, after the gallows seemed to have served for the last time, a "bummer" by the name of Davey Morgan lived in Bannack. He was a moocher and generally a pest around town, but fairly harmless. Finally Davey's mooching had worn really thin. Some of the Vigilantes, as a joke, warned Davey that he had better mend his ways and find some purpose to life, otherwise he would meet the same fate as Plummer. Old Davey Morgan took them seriously, sneaked up to the gallows under cover of darkness, and proceeded to chop the gallows off about three feet above the ground. The next day, Morgan, drunk as usual, cheerfully admitted to the deed, gloating that now the Vigilantes would not be able to hang him.

Incidentally, Davey Morgan first staggers into the pages of history on the night of January 12, 1864. A.J. "Ajax" Noyes relates in *The Story of Ajax* that William Roe (the Vigilante who led the capture of Buck Stinson) was passing by the unfinished building where Dutch John Wagner was still hanging from the rafters. Roe saw a light flicker on and off in the room and for a moment was startled. Upon investigating, he found little Davey Morgan—very, very intoxicated—as he stood there striking matches, "jus' to take a look at the bloody bugger!"

did amidst Mrs. Vail's questions. Plummer told her that they just wanted to talk to him about Dutch John Wagner, and left with the group of determined men.

The three companies met at the gallows. The night was extremely cold, and the men had a very unsavory job to do, so they did not waste any time. Ned Ray was the first hanged, followed by Buck Stinson—both men spewing epithets every step of the way. Plummer was not the big tough leader he pretended to be. He begged for his life, then changed his tactics and stated that he was too wicked to die. Finally he resigned himself to the fate of joining his cohorts on the gallows in death. After tossing the kerchief from around his neck to a young friend, he requested the Vigilantes to give him a good drop. His request was granted, and he was lifted as high as several men could, and dropped into eternity. The 27-year-old outlaw sheriff's dark career and life were over.

A guard was placed to keep people away from the swinging corpses. After about an hour, the guard left, satisfied that the last breath of life had left the three outlaws. Their bodies were taken down the next day. However, burial in Boot Hill, located just above the gallows at the top of the hill, would be unheard of since the townspeople did not want such vile men lying in perpetual slumber with their loved ones. Shallow graves were dug not far from where the men had spent the last moments of their lives.

The Vigilantes went on to hang the rest of the Road Agents that they could locate, in such locations as Hellgate (Missoula), Cottonwood (Deer Lodge), Fort Owen and Virginia City. The accounts state that all told, 32 men were either hanged or banished, with only three receiving that second chance. One hundred and two documented murders by the Road Agents had taken place, along with an unknown number of robberies.

Reports abound about the fabulous loot that Plummer and his gang amassed,

giving rise to the legend of Henry Plummer's treasure. The other side of the story, probably more realistic, is that the Road Agents spent the loot as fast as they could get it on whisky, gambling and women of dubious character.

The Vigilantes were spurred on by their success and general public approval. They decided to seek other law breakers and deal with them as they saw fit until a competent judiciary should be established.

On the morning following the execution of Plummer and his deputies, the Bannack Vigilance Committee decided to investigate the "career" of Joe Pizanthia, the only Mexican in the camp. Pizanthia had brought with him the reputation of being a robber, desperado and murderer. His activities at Bannack were also under suspicion, so the Vigilantes—accompanied by a group of onlookers—went to Pizanthia's cabin, located against a small hill on Bannack's south side. George Copley and Smith Ball led the public group. Upon arrival at the cabin they called for the suspected outlaw to come out. He refused, so the two men, against friends' advice, cautiously lifted the

doorlatch and entered the cabin. Two shots rang out, both hitting their marks. Copley was hit in the breast. Led off by two friends, he died soon afterwards. Ball received a superficial wound in the hip. The crowd was incensed that Pizanthia would dare to shoot these two popular men. After Copley's death was announced, the crowd was enraged to near

Above: The footbridge crossing Grasshopper Creek from Bannack into where Yankee Flat was located. Today the bridge begins one of the most beautiful (unguided) walks in Bannack State Park.
Left: The site of Rattlesnake Stage Station, another hangout of the Road Agents, is 15 miles from Bannack on the northbound stage road. Mt. Baldy is a magnificent sight up Rattlesnake Creek from where the stage station once stood. Road Agent Red Yeager was captured in a wickiup in the willows about 100 yards from that station, also called Parish, Bunton and Co. after its owners.

MR. & MRS. HENRY PLUMMER

Henry Plummer...the man is certainly an enigma of the Old West. Some historians assert that Henry Plummer was an alias for a man whose real name has been lost in the mists of time. However, Art Pauley wrote a very well-researched book on Henry Plummer that traces his origins to a farm near Houlton, Maine as the son of Rial and Roseanna Plummer. Rial and family, along with Henry's brother Ed, relocated in Sauk County, Wisconsin.

In 1852, Amos Henry Plummer is traced to Nevada City, California, where he ultimately entered the bakery business and local law enforcement as city marshal. Five years later, he got into a shooting scrape over a woman, and was charged in the death of her husband, John Vedder. The jury rendered a verdict of murder in the second degree.

A second trial was granted, with the venue changed to Yuba City, California. Again came a guilty verdict, and Henry was sentenced to 10 years in San Quentin.

Plummer began serving his sentence on February 22, 1859 as inmate number 1573. Among his comrades behind bars was Cyrus Skinner, serving time for grand larceny.

Plummer served time only until August 16, 1859, when he was released because of a supposedly fatal illness. Plummer returned to Nevada City, California, where a friend appointed him city constable. But he was "unappointed" after his friend lost the next election.

Plummer remained out of trouble until February of 1861 when he nearly killed a man in a fight. Then on the following October 27, Plummer got into a shooting match at a local house of ill fame and killed one William Riley. Plummer was incarcerated, but escaped only five days later by literally running out the door. He hid with friends in Carson City, and finally went to Lewiston, Idaho where he and a woman companion registered at the Luna House in January 1862.

In Lewiston Plummer ran into his old cellmate, Cyrus Skinner, and other individuals destined for the gallows in Montana, such as Club Foot George Lane and Bill Bunton. Plummer abandoned his mistress, a woman with three children who had to resort to prostitution to feed herself and family, and finally died an alcoholic and "an inmate in one of the lowest dives in town." Roaming the area between Elk City, Florence and Lewiston, Plummer became a wanted man again, this time for the death of Patrick Ford.

This time the outlaw ended up at Sun River, Montana in November 1862, where he met his future wife, Electa Bryan, who was staying with her sister and brother-in-law, Martha and James Vail. Also at Sun River, he became reacquainted with Jack Cleveland, a fellow just as unscrupulous as Plummer.

Plummer ended up in Bannack, where he was appointed sheriff. Henry and Electa were married in Sun River on June 20, 1863 by Jesuit priest Fr. Joseph Menetry in St. Peter's Mission. The newlyweds arrived in Bannack four days later to make their home, but in less than three months, Electa left for Cedar Rapids, Iowa, where her parents lived. Her reason for leaving never will be known. Theories purport that she finally got to know Henry Plummer and left because she disapproved of his violent nature and life of crime, or even that she left Bannack with the expectation that Henry Plummer would join her in the spring.

Electa ultimately moved to Vermillion, South Dakota, where she married James Maxwell, a widower with two daughters. Electa and James had two sons of their own, Vernon and Clarence. Electa lived until May 5, 1912. She was buried at Wakonda, South Dakota.

madness. Popular sentiment was for summary justice. A mountain howitzer, with a bore of 4.52 inches, left at Bannack by a wagon train, was brought to the site. Three shells were directed at the luckless cabin from which Pizanthia refused to emerge—the last at the chimney, where it was supposed Pizanthia was hiding.

Vigilante John Lott and a small party finally stormed the dwelling, and saw the hunted man's boots protruding from under the door, which had fallen in upon him. Pizanthia, badly injured, was dragged forth. Smith Ball, as soon as he saw Pizanthia, emptied his six-shot revolver into him. The corpse was hanged on a pole, using a clothesline as a hangman's rope. As the lifeless corpse dangled, it was reported, the angry crowd discharged more than 100 shots into it.

The mob set fire to Pizanthia's cabin, and tossed his body onto the makeshift pyre. Nothing at all remained of the outlaw, and little of his cabin save for a pile of charred timbers. The next morning, as the reports state, a gathering of "notorious" women unsuccessfully panned the ashes in search of gold.

The Pizanthia episode was the action of a mob instead of the Vigilance Committee, since the Vigilantes involved wanted nothing more than to question the man about his actions and his knowledge of illegal activities. Vigilante chronicler Nathaniel Pitt Langford reflected the moral dilemma of the unfortunate occurrence: "This entire transaction was an act of popular vengeance. The people were infuriated at the murder of Copley, who, besides being one of their best citizens, was a general favorite. There seemed to be no occasion or excuse for it, as the Vigilantes contemplated nothing more by the arrest of Pizanthia than an examination of his territorial record. With the crimes he had committed before he came to the Territory, they had nothing to do; and if he had been guilty of none after he came there, the heaviest possible punishment they would have inflicted was banish-

ment. He brought his fate upon himself. It was a brief interlude in Vigilante history, the terrible features of which, though they may be deemed without apology or excuse, need not seek for multiplied precedents outside of the most enlightened nations or most refined societies in all Christendom."

The evening of Pizanthia's death, January 11, the Vigilance Committee met again, and the case of Dutch John Wagner came under discussion. The committee unanimously felt that Dutch John should be hanged for his life as a Road Agent, and they proceeded to inform him so. He quickly wrote a letter in German to his mother, and prepared to face his death. He was marched to an unfinished building where the frozen bodies of Plummer and Stinson had been laid out, one on the floor and the other on a bench. (Ned Ray's body had since been claimed by his mistress, Madame Hall, and taken for burial.) Vigilantes threw a rope over a crossbeam, and placed a barrel for the condemned man to stand upon. The noose was adjusted around his neck, and another rope put around the head of the barrel. At the command, "All ready," the rope was jerked, sending Dutch John Wagner to his sudden death.

The reign of terror of the Road Agents lasted for 16 months, from the time Plummer came to Bannack about November 1, 1862 until February of 1864 when the last of the Road Agents was hanged.

Road Agent Rock, located about three miles from Bannack on the stage road to Virginia City, was used by Road Agents looking out for stagecoaches and horseback riders to rob. The large outcropping afforded a good view in all directions as well as concealment for horses.

THE GRAVE OF PLUMMER AND ASSOCIATES

The exact locations of the gallows and grave of Henry Plummer are mysteries, as well as what happened exactly to his skeleton.

After the outlaw sheriff was hanged with two of his cohorts on January 10, 1864, the bodies were taken to an unfinished building on Main Street across from the Goodrich Hotel (adjacent to and just east of Skinner's Saloon), where they lay for a day. One account states that Madame Hall, Ned Ray's mistress, took his body to her cabin and arranged for the burial herself. Plummer and Stinson were laid out on a bench and the floor, respectively. On the next evening, in the same unfinished building, Dutch John Wagner was hanged by Vigilantes from a crossbeam, and his body placed with those of the other Road Agents.

On the 13th of January, the four bodies (by that time Madame Hall had returned the body of Ned Ray, if she ever had claimed it) were taken and buried in a common grave just to the right of where the gallows replica stands up Hangman's Gulch. Only Plummer had the luxury of being buried in a coffin. (One account states that Stinson and Ray were buried in Boot Hill on the hill east of the gallows.)

The grave of the four Road Agents had not been very deep, for the ground was frozen hard, and no one wanted to work very hard to bury the outlaws. Hangman's Gulch, where the burial took place, is often disturbed by flash floods that rearrange the landscape and its contents. Undoubtedly some of what was buried in the Road Agents' grave washed away in the numerous floods that have rampaged down the gulch.

Local legend tells two tales about the fate of Henry Plummer's skull. The first, and most probable, says that two drunks, about the turn of the century, dug up Plummer's skull and deposited it on the backbar of Bannack's Bank Exchange Saloon. There the curious relic reposed until the saloon burned and, with it, all its contents. The second story is undoubtedly just that, a story, but is nevertheless fascinating. This account relates that the same old drunks dug up the skull, which finally found its way into the hands of a Bannack doctor. The unnamed doctor sent the specimen "back east to a scientific institution for study to try to figure out why Plummer was so evil."

The Bank Exchange Saloon was a popular "watering-hole" in Bannack, with the upstairs a house of ill repute. Henry Plummer's skull was reported to have been kept on the backbar and was destroyed when the bar burned in 1906.
PHOTO COURTESY DONNA LANDA

The Vigilantes' work was swift and sure, and ended as quickly as it began. They were men who were honest and hardworking, and who realized that in order for the Territory to be a safe place in which to live and to raise a family, law and order had to be instilled in the gold camps. Needless to say, the calming effect of the Vigilantes on southwestern Montana was felt for many years to come.

Facing page: The first of two Bannack cemeteries, overlooking Hangman's Gulch and the gallows, saw its first burial early in 1863. With most of the graves now unmarked, the Trask family marker watches over an elevated plot.

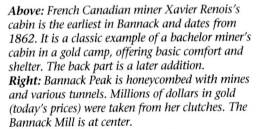

Above: French Canadian miner Xavier Renois's cabin is the earliest in Bannack and dates from 1862. It is a classic example of a bachelor miner's cabin in a gold camp, offering basic comfort and shelter. The back part is a later addition.
Right: Bannack Peak is honeycombed with mines and various tunnels. Millions of dollars in gold (today's prices) were taken from her clutches. The Bannack Mill is at center.

Above: *Bannack State Park is a bird watcher's paradise. Barn swallows* (Hirundo rustica) *nest in various houses and are a welcome addition to the multitude of birds seen throughout the year.*
Left: *Bannack's Masonic Temple was home to Bannack Lodge No. 16, A.F. & A.M. until declining membership forced consolidation with Dillon's Masonic Lodge in 1921.*

Above: The Ryburn House, built about 1896, was home to Bannack physician Robert Ryburn, and continued as a residence until the 1960s.
Right: The prairie rattlesnake (Crotalus viridis) *lies curled in self-protection after being startled. Although not commonly found at Bannack due to the elevation, rattlers are seen occasionally, especially in hot, dry summers.*

Facing page: Hoar frost seems to deepen the 40-below temperature. Limestone cliffs in the background overshadow a barn built about 1896.

Above: The gallus frame, a silent reminder of mining activity at Bannack, once was used to hoist ore and rock out of a mine shaft.
Right: Fragile prickly pear cactus (Opuntia fragilis), which covers the ground at Bannack, once was used by the Indians as a food.
Far right: The barrenness of late autumn makes the once comfortable Graves house fit into the now-austere mood at Bannack. Built about 1867, the Graves house is said to be the first frame house in Montana. Owned by Fielding L. Graves, for whom the electric gold dredge was named, the spacious home once boasted a crystal chandelier in the parlor.

Overleaf: Dr. Robert Ryburn's office and the Meade Hotel.

Above: *This cabin was once the home of the French family and is now the Visitor Center. Carpenter George French built Henry Plummer's coffin, for which he was paid $42.50.*

Left: *Most miners who moved to Bannack did not want to spend a lot of time building a cabin, so many roomed at such places as the Gibson House (foreground), run by Archie Gibson and his wife Maggie. Reportedly built in the 1860s, this building "roomed and boarded" many of Bannack's miners through the years.*

Facing page: *The Graeter House was owned by Augustus F. Graeter, for whom Bannack's third and largest gold dredge was named. The rock fireplace was built by unknown hands and is a fine example of early talent in the camp.*

Bannack Peak looms over Main Street as another day dawns on the Grasshopper. Many of the gaps on Bannack's street are the result of fires through the years, as well as buildings being torn down for lumber or firewood. The third building from right is Crisman's Store, owned by George Crisman. One of the most popular places in Bannack, it was described as "the news bureau, the university, the social settlement of the hamlet to which intelligent, genial companionship and a wide fireplace gave cheerful welcome," by Wilbur Fisk Sanders.

Above: *Bannack's church was built in 1877 under the direction of Methodist missionary "Brother Van," William Van Orsdel. Construction was suspended on the house of worship for a few days when rumors abounded that Chief Joseph and his Nez Perce were about to attack Bannack.*
Left: *A mule deer grazes in the yard of the Mathews House, built in 1886, sharing tranquility with the camp and the visitor fortunate to come along at the right time.*

Overleaf: *Montana's state flower, the bitterroot* (Lewisia rediviva), *adds a silent beauty to the landscape of Montana and to Bannack's surrounding hills during summer. Its scientific name honors Meriwether Lewis.*

ROAD AGENTS

Brady, James—Hanged January 15, 1864 at Virginia City.

Brown, George W.—Hanged with Red Yeager January 4, 1864 at Lorrain's on the banks of the Passamari (Ruby) River. Said that he had an Indian wife and family in Minnesota.

Bunton, Bill—Hanged January 19, 1864 in the Deer Lodge Valley. A native of Ohio. His parents moved to Andrew County, Missouri in 1839, and thence to Oregon in 1842. Born in 1826. Ran the the Rattlesnake Stage Station on Rattlesnake Creek located "up" from the Stone House. Reportedly the second in command of the Road Agents.

Bunton, Sam—Bill Bunton's brother, expelled from the gang for allegedly being a drunkard.

Carter, Alex— Hanged January 25, 1864 at Hellgate. He helped Ives and Irwin take Tiebalt's mules to Irwin's ranch in the Big Hole.

Cleveland, Jack—Shot in Goodrich Saloon by Henry Plummer in January of 1863 because he knew too much of Plummer's past. According to one source, his real name was John Farnsworth, and he was born in New York state in 1828. He had moved with his family to Jo Daviess County, Illinois where he grew up.

Cooper, Johnny—Hanged January 25, 1864 at Hellgate. His parents lived in New York. He came from the Willamette Valley in Oregon.

Crowell, Tex—Captured with Bill Bunton, tried and released due to inconclusive evidence.

Forbes, Charley—The probable slayer of Deputy Dillingham. Possibly killed by Haze Lyons and Buck Stinson.

Franck, Long John—Banished December 1863. "Roomed" with Hilderman.

Gallagher, Jack—Hanged January 14, 1864 in Virginia City and buried at Boot Hill.

Graves, Whiskey Bill—Hanged January 26, 1864 at Fort Owen.

Helm, Boone—Hanged January 14, 1864 in Virginia City and buried at Boot Hill. A native of Kentucky. His parents emigrated to one of the newest settlements in Missouri when he was a boy. Married in 1848 and had a daughter in Monroe County, Missouri. Killed a man and was committed to a lunatic asylum. He escaped and fled to California. He admitted to being a cannibal. He had three brothers who went to the Pacific Coast between 1848 and 1850, and all met violent deaths.

Hilderman, George—Banished after the Ives trial due to his old age. Known as the "Great American Pie Biter."

Howard, Daniel "Doc"—Born in 1830 in New York City as David Renton. He was called Doc because he had taken some courses in a medical school. He served time in San Quentin prison for grand larceny. The ringleader of the Magruder robbery and murder committed with Romaine and Lowery. Executed March 4, 1864 in Lewiston, Idaho with the other two killers after a short trial.

Hunter, William—Hanged February 3, 1864 in Gallatin County about 20 miles above the mouth of the Gallatin. He was the last of Plummer's band to be executed.

Ives, George—Hanged December 21, 1863 at Nevada City for the murder of Nicholas Tiebalt. Left a mother and sisters in Wisconsin. He was a miner in California in 1857-58. His first recorded instance of criminal activity was stealing government mules at Walla Walla, Washington.

Lane, Club Foot George—Hanged January 14, 1864 at Virginia City and buried at Boot Hill.

Lowery, Chris—Involved in the robbery and murder of Lloyd Magruder. Allegedly killed Magruder with an axe. Executed March 4, 1864 in Lewiston, Idaho. Originally from Pennsylvania, he hired on as a blacksmith with the Mullan Expedition. Served three years of a five year sentence in San Quentin for grand larceny, then escaped from prison and left California for good.

Lyons, Haze—Hanged January 14, 1864 at Virginia City and buried at Boot Hill.

Marshland, Steve—Hanged January 16, 1864 in the Big Hole Valley at Clarke's Big Hole Ranch.

Page, Billy—He grew up and attended school in Oregon. Banished from Bannack due to his youth. Went to Lewiston, Idaho where he "stood state's evidence" in the Lloyd Magruder murder case. He was killed Christmas Day of 1866 by Al Igo after Page beat him up in a fight.

Parish, Frank—Hanged January 14, 1864 at Virginia City and buried at Boot Hill.

Pizanthia, Joe—Killed January 11, 1864 at Bannack. Burned in his cabin after being shot and hanged by a mob.

Plummer, Henry—Hanged January 10, 1864 at Bannack along with his Road Agent deputies, Buck Stinson and Ned Ray.

Ray, Ned—Hanged January 10, 1864 at Bannack with Henry Plummer and Buck Stinson. The first one to be hanged.

Romaine, James—In Marysville, California he had worked as a contractor, and in The Dalles, as a gambler. Hanged with Howard and Lowery on March 4, 1864 in Lewiston, Idaho for the Magruder robbery and murders.

Shears, George—Hanged January 24, 1864 at Frenchtown.

Skinner, Cyrus—Hanged January 25, 1864 at Hellgate. Proprietor of Skinner's Saloon at Bannack, the reported "headquarters" of the Road Agents.

Terwilliger, Billy—Named by Red Yeager as a member of Plummer's band. He left the area before being apprehended.

Stinson, I.N. "Buck"—Hanged January 10, 1864.

Wagner, Dutch John—Hanged January 11, 1864 at Bannack.

Yeager, Erastus (Red)—Hanged January 4, 1864 from an old cottonwood tree at Lorrain's (now Laurin) on the banks of the Passamari (Ruby) River.

Zachary, Bob—Hanged January 26, 1864 at Hellgate.

Top: Bannack during the height of the dredging period, about 1899, shows the large ponds that the F.L. Graves dredge needed in which to operate.
Above: Started by the French family in the 1860s, the Bannack Brewery was sold to James Harly in 1870.

CAPITAL CITY

President Abraham Lincoln appointed Sidney Edgerton as Chief Justice of Idaho Territory, where Bannack was located. Arriving in Bannack in September of 1863, Edgerton saw at once that this newly-made territory was too vast to be administered from the capital of Lewiston. He drew up plans for a new territory to be carved from the eastern portion of Idaho Territory. With the proper petitions in hand, he convinced President Lincoln to create Montana Territory.

After much heated Congressional discussion over what the new territory should be called, on May 26, 1864, President Lincoln signed into law the 1864 Organic Act creating Montana Territory, and appointed Sidney Edgerton its first governor.

When Governor Edgerton returned to Bannack, he immediately set about organizing the territory. As the population center (and home to the governor's family), Bannack was chosen as the capital. The town had been named for the Bannock Indians who lived in the area. Why the difference in the spelling (Bann*a*ck City and Bann*o*ck Indians)? One story states that Governor Edgerton sent legal papers to President Lincoln regarding the formation of the new Territory of Montana and detailed its capital as Bannock. However, the president's secretary had some difficulty in reading Governor Edgerton's handwriting, and entered the spelling as Bannack on legal documents. By the time the mistake was discovered, it would have been too much legal work to change the spelling, so it was left as Bannack. Another popular story states that the mistake in spelling was

made by the U.S. Post Office when the first office was set up at Bannack in the 1860s.

The first legislature in Montana Territory, which lasted about 60 days, was bicameral and met in separate structures in Bannack. The exact location of the buildings is unknown. However, from early descriptions the two buildings seem to have been on either side of where the Meade Hotel is now. The first session of the Legislature was called to order by Judge L.P. Williston at noon on December 12, 1864. The two houses met in joint session for the opening and then reconvened in their separate quarters.

The upper house consisted of a seven-member council, and the lower house of 13 members. During the session, Francis M. Thompson—Bannack resident and Beaverhead County delegate—designed the official territorial seal, which was adopted February 5, 1865. Thompson's design was used for the Great Seal of the State of Montana in 1889, and stands today.

That first legislature passed a large volume of hastily written laws, mainly dealing with roads, public schools, voter eligibility, irrigation and mining. One law provided for registration of brands in the territory's eight existing counties, with

strict penalties for altering or duplicating registered brands—demonstrating the importance cattle ranching already held.

During the first 16 months of existence, Montana did not have a territorial secretary. Since only the secretary could sign federal warrants, no federal funds could be spent. Governor Edgerton paid for much of the cost of government from his own pocket, expecting to be reimbursed by the federal government. When such money did not come, he left for the east to tend to Montana's affairs in Washington and also to his own affairs in Ohio. He was forced to resign in 1866,

Top: The "Governor's Mansion" was a log building that Governor Edgerton purchased for $400 as his family home. The building burned in the 1920s. Bannack miner Amede Bessette, right, is holding Plummer's shotgun, which he owned for many years. Above: Built from the logs of the "Governor's Mansion" about 1940, this building stands approximately at the original location of Governor Edgerton's home.

MEADE HOTEL

Much of the building historically known as the Hotel Meade was designed by architect Loren B. Olds. It was built in 1875-1876 as the first Beaverhead County Courthouse at a cost of $14,000. The bricks were handmade locally.

In August of 1877, townspeople fortified the building against possible attack by Chief Joseph and his band of Nez Perce who had just fought the Battle of the Big Hole.

When the county seat was moved to Dillon in 1882, the building was remodeled and opened as a hotel with an extensive addition to the rear. The Meade family eventually gained full ownership of the building, which served as hotel, restaurant and assay office. In 1895, the Meade Hotel was remodeled and reopened with a good livery and feed stable under the proprietorship of John S. Meade. The fare was $2.50 per day or $7.00 per week. In the 1920s an addition onto the back provided rooms for many miners. In 1931 the I.B. Mining Company bought the hotel and located their company offices there while still supplying miners' rooms. The state of Montana acquired the hotel in 1954.

largely due to a political disagreement with President Andrew Johnson.

By 1865, Bannack's population had shifted to other gold camps, such as Helena and Alder Gulch. The politicians felt that, since Bannack was no longer the territory's population center, the seat of government should be changed, and they opted for Virginia City. Therefore, on February 7, 1865, Virginia City formally became the capital of Montana Territory and remained so until it suffered the same fate 10 years later and Helena was named capital on April 19, 1875.

Above: *Looking north at Bannack about 1890, showing how extensive the town was then.*
Left: *Bannack's Main Street before 1896 showing the Meade Hotel, Skinner's Saloon, the Bannack Hotel and a livery stable. Formerly the Goodrich Hotel, the Bannack Hotel was the first hotel in Montana. It was ultimately moved to Virginia City and became the Fairweather Inn in the 1950s. Episcopal missionary Bishop Daniel Tuttle preached his first sermon in Bannack from this balcony in 1867.*

Lemhi chief Tendoy and one of his many children. His aunt was Sacajawea of Lewis and Clark fame.

INDIANS

Indians, primarily the Lemhis, were frequent visitors in the town of Bannack and were generally received well. Many of the young Indian children played with their white counterparts, and developed life-long friendships. Later, the Nez Perce under Chief Joseph contributed an interesting chapter to Bannack's history. Let us begin with the Lemhi story.

Chief Snag was a chief among the Lemhi Indians, respected both by whites and Indians alike. His paternal aunt was Sacajawea of the Lewis and Clark expedition, and his uncle Chief Cameahwait. Snag had been a chief many years and had often come to Bannack to trade for food and goods. During the spring of 1863, Snag and several others, among them his nephew Tendoy, were below Bannack on the banks of Grasshopper Creek. Snag decided to bathe in the cool stream. Road Agent Buck Stinson rode up with several of his cohorts and proceeded to shoot the chief dead—apparently Stinson's perverse idea of amusement. Tendoy and the other Indians escaped. Later Tendoy was chosen chief to replace his uncle. In spite of Snag's murder, Chief Tendoy and the Lemhis continued to visit Bannack and, eventually, Dillon. They were popular participants in parades for many years. Chief Tendoy died in 1907.

The Nez Perce were Washington residents who fled their homeland rather than move onto an Idaho reservation in 1877. Unfortunately, about 20 young warriors attacked white settlers along the way, in mid-June, and the U.S. Army gave pursuit. Tribal leaders decided to head for Crow country, against the wishes of one junior leader, Chief Joseph.

In July, the tribe crossed over Lolo Pass into the Bitterroot Valley of western Montana. They traveled into the Big Hole Valley and made camp along its banks, in an apparently safe location. On August 9, just before dawn, Colonel John Gibbon attacked the sleeping village and killed nearly 90 people, mainly women and children. Battle was waged all day, with the Nez Perce definitely gaining the upper hand. The next night, Joseph and his people slipped away under cover of darkness and headed south toward Yellowstone National Park.

In Bannack, rumors were rampant that Chief Joseph was going to attack the town and murder everyone in retaliation for the attack in the Big Hole. Townspeople barricaded women and children in the brick courthouse (now the Meade Hotel), several young girls staying in the two large safes. Men of Bannack made small rock and wood forts on each side of the hills surrounding the entrance to Hangman's Gulch, from which they hoped to protect

the town. On August 12, the Nez Perce were seen heading south down Grasshopper Valley toward Horse Prairie. Joseph, his heart sick at the trouble with whites whom he considered friends, had no intention whatever of attacking Bannack, and least of all of murdering women and children.

Finally, on October 5, 1877, failing to reach the safety of the Canadian border, Chief Joseph surrendered to Colonel Nelson A. Miles near present-day Chinook, Montana, promising, "From where the sun now stands, I will fight no more forever."

MINING

Mining has always been the main attraction at Bannack. Ever since John White and his fellow prospectors found gold on the Grasshopper in 1862, gold has lured more men to Bannack than anything else. By the same token, Bannack *lost* more men to gold—because gold lured men to new strikes such as Alder Gulch at Virginia City and Nevada City, Last Chance Gulch at Helena, to the mines at

Salmon, Idaho and even to the Yukon and Alaska.

At first men came with picks and shovels and panned for gold, which is placer mining at its most rudimentary. If the diggings looked promising, miners constructed rockers, fashioned after baby cradles. The rectangular rocker had sides about two feet high, which sifted the gravel. Finer, gold-bearing gravel then was panned and the gold extracted.

Miners also set up sluice boxes, board troughs with crossboards called riffles in the bottom. A stream of water washed gravel through the sluice, with the much heavier gold sinking to the bottom and being trapped by the riffles.

Another common form of mining used at Bannack—even today—is hydraulic mining. High-pressure hoses wash dirt and gravel from hillsides to sluices below, and the gravel then is sluiced for gold. Much evidence of hydraulic mining is seen above and below Bannack—deep cuts in the hillsides that look as though flash floods came through the area.

One of the most productive forms of mining at Bannack was dredging, which

Joe Gauthier and Frenchy Rossie hydraulic mining below Bannack.

Above: The Golden Leaf Mill was built below Bannack about 1890 at a cost of nearly $60,000 and employed 50 to 60 men in its electrically lighted operation. The flume provided water from miles away.

Right: In a heavily doctored old photograph, Tom Thompson and John Steger rock gold at Bannack.

lasted from 1895 until approximately 10 years later. A total of five dredge boats worked Grasshopper Creek and dug as deep as 40 feet looking for gold. Since bedrock was known to be deep in Grasshopper Gulch, no one was sure that even a dredge could reach it until H. J. Reiling of Chicago, and others, organized the Gold Dredging Company and built the first boat, the *Fielding L. Graves*, in 1895. It was the first electric dredge in the world.

The dredge's machinery was built by the Bucyrus Steam Shovel and Dredge Company of Milwaukee, and moved by a spur line of the Union Pacific, the Utah and Northern Railroad, to Red Rock, Montana. The heavy machinery was then freighted by teams and wagons for 40 miles to Bannack, and the boat was constructed on Bannack's east end at a cost of about $35,000.

Water was run more than 30 miles by the Graves-Graeter ditch to power the hydroelectric plant on the banks of Grasshopper Creek 350 feet below the ditch. This plant powered the *F. L. Graves* for the seven years that it worked Grasshopper Creek.

The dredge was launched May 15, 1895 with a large celebration culminating with the wife of the Gold Dredging Company's president breaking a bottle of champagne on its bow and christening the boat after one of Bannack's pioneer merchants. The *F.L. Graves* immediately began operation, its crew of pilot, motorman and deckhand working six months of the year—the normal dredging season, determined by ice on the creek. The corporation purchased about two miles of the Grasshopper's bed for the dredge to work.

Buckets, each weighing 1,200 pounds and holding five cubic feet of gravel, dumped their loads into a sluice box on the dredge itself. Water was then run through the sluice, leaving gold-bearing dirt caught in the riffles. At the end of the "run," the gravel was removed and panned, yielding between $800 and $7,000 per weekly cleanup. The largest

cleanups recorded were $22,000 and $38,000 in two successive weeks' work. The dredge operated until 1902 when it "ran out of auriferous gravel." Its remains still are visible west of Bannack on the Grasshopper, where it was moored in 1902.

In April of 1896, Edward L. Smith of Gilman, Smith and Co. began work on a second dredge at Marysville about $1\frac{1}{2}$ miles below Bannack. On Saturday, May 23, 1897 the *Maggie A. Gibson* was christened by Maggie (Mrs. Archie) Gibson. The *Maggie A. Gibson* began work on July 27, 1896, and was remodeled in the spring of 1897. It operated successfully for two seasons. The lease on the ground ran out in 1898, and within the year this dredge was relocated to the Conrey placers at the mouth of Alder Gulch.

The third and largest Bannack dredge, the *A.F. Graeter*, was launched at Marysville on April 14, 1897. In its first year of operation, the 36'-by-102' dredge with its 36 buckets recovered $20,000 in gold. The Bannack Dredging Company owned and operated the *A. F. Graeter*, fueled by eight cords of wood per day. It ceased operation in 1902 and was dormant until 1906 when

An early mine at Bannack with headframe and tracks for ore cars.

Right: The Coast—*Owned by the Coast Dredging Company of New Jersey. Also called* The Cope *because C.F. Cope of Helena sold the company the land on which it operated (1898-1902).*

Below: Maggie A. Gibson—*Christened at Marysville by Mrs. Archie (Maggie A.) Gibson on May 23, 1897. Worked a short time on the Grasshopper (1896-1898), then moved to the Conrey Placers at Alder Gulch .*

Facing page, above right: Schematic drawing of a mining dredge.

Above left: Bon Accord—*This dredge operated only a few days in September 1897 until, owing to its top-heavy design, it tipped over. The machinery was bought in 1901 by the Oregon Placer Mining Company and moved to the John Day River in Oregon. Its buckets were the largest of all Bannack dredges, nine cubic feet.*

Below: F. L. Graves—*The first electric dredge in the world and first successful bucket-lift dredge in the United States, as well as Bannack's first dredge (1895-1902). Shortly after its launch, its bucket size was increased from $1\frac{1}{2}$ to 5 cubic feet.*

ABOVE AND BELOW: BEAVERHEAD COUNTY MUSEUM PHOTOS

50

DREDGES

Grasshopper Creek at Bannack saw five dredges claw at the gravel and dirt in the creekbed during the dredging period, 1895 until 1902. Bucyrus-Erie of Milwaukee made most of the machinery of the large boats, which was brought by railroad to Red Rock then freighted by wagon to construction sites at Bannack.

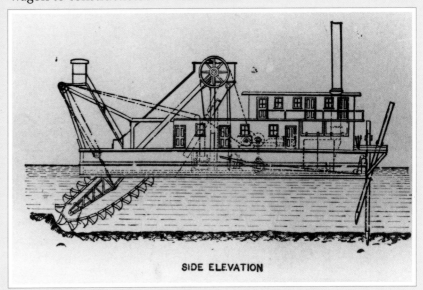

SIDE ELEVATION

BEAVERHEAD COUNTY MUSEUM PHOTO

Above: These old-timers of Bannack spent most of their time sitting on the front porch of the F. L. Graves Store discussing the "good old days" at Bannack. They were jokingly referred to as the Society of the Watchers of the Gulch. From left to right: Fielding L. Graves, Sr., George Gauthier, Amede Bessette, Archie Gibson (standing), Xavier Renois, Frank Gauthier, and Ike Wright.

Right: The A.F. Graeter's final resting place is in Grasshopper Creek across from the parking lot. Moored in 1906, all that is left of the dredge are several planks and dredge buckets.

it was bought by F.B. Felt of Chicago, who operated it briefly on some of the ground previously worked by the *F.L. Graves.* In the fall of 1906, the *A.F. Graeter* was dismantled west of Bannack and its remains left in the creek.

The fourth dredge at Bannack, the *Bon Accord,* was something of a disaster. An English company, the Bon Accord Company, began building the dredge during the fall of 1897, two or three miles below Bannack. The boat had nine-cubic-foot buckets, which would have been the largest capacity of any of the Bannack dredges. But the *Bon Accord* operated only a few days after it was launched, and tipped over because it was top heavy. In 1902, the Oregon Placer Company bought the machinery and moved it to the John Day River, leaving the hulk by Grasshopper Creek.

The fifth dredge was called the *Coast* or the *Cope.* In the summer of 1898, the Montana Gold Dredging Company began work on this dredge near Spring Creek, about one mile downstream from the *Bon Accord.* It was named the *Coast* after its owners, the Coast Dredging Company of Monmouth, New Jersey. It was also called the *Cope* after George F. Cope, a Helena banker who sold the land upon which the dredge was built. This dredge worked the Grasshopper below Bannack until 1902 when it was dismantled near the *Bon Accord.* The *Coast* was reported to have recovered 19,194 ounces of gold.

Several mining companies developed hardrock, or underground, mines at Bannack, including the Gold Bug, Wallace, Golden Leaf, Excelsior, Eugenia and the Hendricks. The Excelsior mine is reported to have gone to a depth of 300 feet and yielded more than $300,000 in gold. In 1891, the Golden Leaf Company employed more than 50 men in its electrically-lighted mill and mines. The Golden Leaf mines are estimated to have yielded more than $1.3 million worth of gold. The Golden Leaf Mill, built about 1890, stood on the south side of the Grasshopper three

Built during World War I, the Apex Mill operated into its fifth decade.

THE MAYOR OF BANNACK

Chandler Wellington Stallings was born in Kansas City, Kansas on July 1, 1881. By the time he was 13, both parents and his sister had died, and he was raised by a family friend. Chan went to college in Moscow, Idaho and became a mining engineer. After graduation he packed his gear and his geology books on a mule and headed cross-country to the Bannack Diggins', arriving in 1913. He got a job with the New York Mining Company and spent the next 30 years working for various companies at Bannack, as both mining engineer and promoter. Chan Stallings married Lelah Graves, daughter of Fielding L. Graves, in Bannack on June 3, 1915.

Stallings was superintendent of the Bannack Gold Mining Company, which employed more than 50 men in its mines, when he supervised the crew of 20 constructing its new mill in 1917. Commonly called the Apex Mill today, it stands across the Grasshopper from town.

In 1946, Chan became the Montana Fish and Game Department's caretaker of Bannack, and for the next 20 years he bore the unofficial title of Mayor of Bannack. Much early restoration work here was done by him or under his direction.

Chan excelled at the art of sourdough making and was responsible for "perfecting the perfect" sourdough hotcake.

He retired in 1965 and moved to Dillon. He and Lelah died in 1969, six months apart, at ages 88 and 79 respectively. The couple had jokingly attributed their longevity to the water at Bannack.

Above: No longer standing, this typical one-room miner's cabin at Bannack was cool in the summer and warm in the winter.

Right: The tree that saw the hanging of Plummer: When the Bannack Ditch was dug about 1865 the roots of this tree extended to such a degree that they had to be cut to allow passage of the ditch. Located about half way up Bannack Peak, the tree still is living and bears the scars of many hard winters, as well as man-made scars. It witnessed the hanging of Henry Plummer that cold Sunday evening of January 10, 1864. Mt. Baldy is the snow-capped mountain seen through its spreading branches, and Bannack can be glimpsed to the right of its trunk.

quarters of a mile below Bannack. In 1917, the Bannack Gold Mining and Milling Company, under the direction of mines and mill superintendent Chandler W. (Chan) Stallings, built the present 200-ton cyanide mill.

Water from the Grasshopper powered its 250-horsepower hydroelectric power plant. In 1931, the I. B. Haviland Company took over the mill and mines, and ran 21 miles of electric lines from Dillon to power them. Haviland renamed the mines "The Sleeping Princess," and received $32,000 a month for the gold concentrates at peak production. Since 1934, and under several owners, the mines have not yielded much gold.

The Suffield and Hendricks mines are located directly up Bannack Peak above the mill and were taken over by Chan Stallings in 1918. The Hendricks can be seen as the large hole in the ground directly behind the Bannack Mill. In 1936, Stallings organized the Apex Mining Company, which extracted more than $40,000 from the two mines. Three years later, a miner from Tacoma mined hydraulically west of Bannack, but with little success.

People who could be termed permanent residents of Bannack moved away in the 1940s, when the Grasshopper was thought to be worked out. However, mining has never stopped in the Bannack area since the initial discovery.

Even in the early 1960s, the Spokane National Mines converted the Apex Mill from a cyanide plant to a flotation mill and operated it for a short time. At present, miners still are going over areas already worked, and even are looking at new ground.

The days of abundant gold at Bannack probably are gone. However, as in the mining industry everywhere, present-day Bannack-area miners hold fast to the dream that their bonanza is just in that next shovelful of gravel or in that next load of dirt. And, as in mining everywhere, it just might be…

Above: Organized in 1936 by Chan Stallings, the Apex Mining Company had its offices here on Bannack's south side. The Apex Mill is in the background at the base of Bannack Peak.
Left: Merchant and miner F.L. Graves initially owned the Gold Bug Mine, which continued off and on in operation until recent years, still yielding substantial amounts of gold.

Right: One of many interesting headstones in Bannack's cemetery, William Peck's indicates his fraternal affiliation. The fence around the gravesite was common, to keep wandering cattle and horses off the place of repose.

Facing page: "*If labor is worship, this is a most worshipful community, but of any other kind of worship there is no public manifestation whatever. I verily believe that two-thirds of the people here are infidel and secular.*"—Emily Meredith, who arrived in Bannack in September of 1862.
"*When I come and go to church…I can see card and billiard playing and all the follies carried on during the week have no intermission on Sunday.*"—Lucia Darling, niece of Governor Edgerton.

—BANNACK TODAY—

Bannack today is a state park, a nice, quiet little place with no residents except employees of the Montana Department of Fish, Wildlife and Parks (FWP). Marsh hawks often nest across the Grasshopper behind the jail, and American kestrels nest in openings under the eaves of the Meade Hotel. Red-shafted flickers nest in several trees in the park and are seen busily flying from tree to tree in search of food. Mule deer wander in the meadows around Bannack, and into the campgrounds, on a daily basis—and venture into town at dusk and roam the streets after that last visitor has departed. Beavers and muskrats swimming in the creek are usually quick to avoid any human contact. Large "dirty-faced" squirrels called chickarees are fun to watch in search of food, especially getting into open windows of cars and into packs left on bicycles. Bannack Peak, directly south of town, is home to

Montana's state flower, the bitterroot, as well as many other beautiful species of mountain flora.

Yes, Bannack is a ghost town in the truest sense of the word. It is totally unspoiled by flashy and reckless restoration and raw commercialism. The aim of the FWP is to keep it that way, maintaining Bannack as it was from about 1880 to 1900. Preservation, rather than restoration, is the key word. Men and women of years past came to Bannack to take gold and other riches from her grasp. Today we are fortunate to take from Bannack other riches, and enjoy the beautiful examples of nature, rich memories and a history unrivaled in the Big Sky Country.

Above: Stagecoaches are just one mode of transportation available during Bannack Days.
Right: If you need your horse shoed during Bannack Days, the village blacksmith will oblige.

BANNACK DAYS

Bannack Days traditionally is held the third weekend of July. Events vary from year to year, but all bring history to life.

Several "mountain men" in 1830s period costume set up a black powder shooting gallery up Hangman's Gulch, and let anyone who wishes try their skill at hitting metal targets. Several Indian tipis completely "furnished" accord the visitor a chance to see what a tipi looked like inside. A cavalryman and his lady visit with Bannack visitors and give samples of bannock bread cooked over a campfire in the traditional fry pan. Candle makers are busy in the lot by Skinner's Saloon. Once in a great while, one of the ladies churning butter there will give a lucky person a glass of real buttermilk. Various quilters, weavers and needlework artists, all in 1860s costume, set up demonstrations on the boardwalks. Often beside them is a zither player, or a guitar-strummin' cowboy band softly singing the ballads of yesteryear, such as *Streets of Laredo* or *Clementine*.

Periodically throughout the day there is a staged robbery and shootout, with the bad guy leaving town on the fastest horse available amid the shrieks of the dancehall girls. In various houses, such as the Ryburn House, an 1880s home is temporarily furnished with antiques that could have seen use and life at Bannack more than 100 years ago.

Oftentimes the Masons present their play, *The Vigilantes*, which brings to life such characters as Wilbur Fisk Sanders, Henry Plummer and Ned Ray. The Ma-sons also open the Masonic Temple, giving tours, explaining about Montana's oldest lodge and its various fixtures, and welcoming questions.

Medicine shows, such as Fearless Frog's and Dr. Dick's Medicine Wagon, offer the visitor elixir to sooth and cure everything—including weary muscles, toothaches and hemorrhoids—as he listens to the entertainment.

On Sunday, church services are held in Brother Van's church, where they use gold pans for collection plates. Authentic stagecoaches and old buckboards ferry people on slow, relaxing tours of the camp. Meals can be purchased in the dining room of the Meade Hotel, where the fare oftentimes includes sourdough pancakes, elk chili and buffalo burgers. Bannack Days has something for everyone. Call 406 834-3413 at Bannack, or the Parks Division at Helena (406 444-2535) for more information.

Mountain men set up a shooting table by their tipis and let anyone try his skill at black powder rifles. Metal targets are set up a various distances, and "ping" when hit.

On June 12, 1989, the Montana Centennial Wagon Train left Bannack for Helena, to arrive on July 4, celebrating the 100th anniversary of Montana's becoming the 41st state of the Union. About 50 wagons assembled at the mouth of Hangman's Gulch at the start of the Bannack to Virginia City Road to begin the trek. They traveled via the Ten Mile and Rattlesnake stage stations to Dillon, up the Sweetwater to Virginia City, to Boulder and on to Helena. All kinds of wagons imaginable were on the journey, including Conestogas, chuck wagons, medicine show wagons, buggies and buckboards. Beautiful draft horses and matched pairs of horses and mules pulled the the antique wagons and replicas, many of them handled by men and women in 1860s dress.

SOURDOUGH PANCAKES

STARTER—Put four cups of flour into a large bowl. Empty one package of dry yeast on top of the flour. Measure about four cups of water and stir into the flour and yeast, mixing the batter well. Cover with a plate, and let set overnight in a warm place. (Most kitchens are fine). This is called a sponge and will be the basic sourdough starter to be drawn from again and again.

IN THE MORNING—Take about one cup of starter from the bowl and put into a pint jar. This will be the sponge to be used next time you want sourdough. Refrigerate. This may be kept for 4 to 6 weeks without turning bad.

Into the bowl mix: $1/2$ teaspoon salt, $1/2$ teaspoon sugar, two eggs, and about one tablespoon maple syrup. Approximations are fine. Mix together well. This may be set aside until you are ready to cook, up to a half hour or so. Heat the griddle to medium high heat, or about 350°. When you are ready to cook the pancakes, sprinkle $1/2$ teaspoon baking soda over the batter and mix well. Make pancakes your preferred size. Use all the batter, and freeze the leftover hotcakes, as they reheat well, especially in a microwave.

NEXT TIME—Take the cup of starter sponge out of the refrigerator and put it into a large bowl. Add equal amounts of water and flour, amounts depending on how many people you will be cooking for. Mix well, cover, and put in a warm place for the night. Follow directions above under IN THE MORNING.

CAUTION—If you forget to put aside your next starter sponge after you have added any other ingredient, DO NOT do so at all. A new starter must be made, as a starter made from one to which ingredients have been added other than the basic flour, yeast and water will make you sick.

These hotcakes are some of the best you will ever eat. This recipe is an original from Bannack and is very simple to use. It does not call for a lot of exotic things such as potato water, beer or whatever else tickles the fancy of an imposter sourdough maker. The old timers simply did not have all the extras to put into the mixture, so they closely followed the KISS principle: Keep It Simple, Stupid.

After the fire died out in a Bannack cabin in the winter, the interior turned mighty cold. Temperatures outside sometimes fell to 50 and 60 below in the dead of winter. Since the prospector might not get up every hour on the hour to stoke the fire, the cabin got to be quite cold inside. Indoor temperatures well below freezing would have kept the sourdough from rising for breakfast.

As Bannack legend states, the old prospector would invariably take his sourdough to bed with him to keep it warm so he could brew those fresh hotcakes for his morning partakin's. This was quite common in the gold camps, which is why we are fortunate to have a few ancient starters around today. They have a more mature flavor the older they get. (You will see that too the longer you keep yours). But to get a starter from one with ancient character, or a history if you will, it takes a lot of fast talking and just the right price.

SOURDOUGH CHRONICLES

An old Bannacker was quite active in his church after he moved to Dillon in later years and rose to become the senior warden of the vestry. When their minister decided to leave, it was the duty of the senior warden to chair the replacement search committee. One of the things this old Bannacker liked to do was to invite the prospective minister and his wife to breakfast after church. What better place to get to know someone than over a breakfast of sourdough pancakes! After the minister took his first bite of the famous sourdough hotcake, he would comment how uniquely delightful the hotcake was, and how he had never tasted anything like it before. The old Bannacker would then tell the minister that this was from a special starter that came across the plains by covered wagon into Bannack the year before they hanged Plummer and his Road Agent cohorts. The special starter was traceable to Kentucky before the Civil War, and before that its history was lost in the mists of time. The senior warden would also tell the preacher how his ancestors had to sleep with the starter on winter nights to keep it from freezing, and on and on with the wit and wisdom of sourdough.

One Sunday the old Bannacker had finished his Sourdough Chronicles after interviewing the second or third minister that month. The minister politely listened to the fascinating tales and remarked that the sourdough starter of the old Bannacker was certainly a special one. However, *his* personal starter could claim to be older, as his descended from the one Moses took with him on the Exodus from Egypt into the Holy Land. Needless to say, the old Bannacker cooled his sourdough tales for a while and was thankful when the permanent preacher finally was hired, and he could invite him to dinner rather than breakfast.

THE MOST FREQUENTLY ASKED QUESTIONS AT BANNACK

Bannack's second and "newer" cemetery, about two miles from Bannack as well as from Highway 278, began about 1877 and is still listed as active. This handhewn stone marks the final resting place of one of Bannack's illustrious dead, Frenchman John Cloutier.

1. When did the last people leave Bannack?

The last residents basically left here just prior to World War II when the mining played out. A few people continued to live here until the 1970s, when the state created the park and prohibited other than park personnel from living at Bannack.

2. Can we go into any of the buildings?

Yes, go into anything that is open—most all of the buildings are. The ones that are not open are the shops, storage buildings, and residences of employees.

3. Where did the first Montana Legislature meet?

The exact location is unknown. From local legend and photographs, the buildings stood approximately where the Meade Hotel now stands. Two buildings were used, one for each house of the legislature. Some reports also state that a third building was used as an office for the governor.

4. What is the elevation of Bannack?

The town is 5,780 feet above sea level. The elevation of Bannack Peak (on the southeast side of Bannack) is 7,287 feet.

5. Where is Henry Plummer buried?

It is more accurate to say, where *was* he buried? After he was hanged on January 10, 1864, his corpse along with Buck Stinson's was taken to an unfinished building where they were kept until burial. Plummer was said to have been buried somewhere near the scaffold up a gulch. Most agree that it is somewhere near the present gallows, a replica. The original gallows stood across Hangman's Gulch from the present replica and much nearer to town.

6. Where is Boot Hill?

The original Bannack Cemetery is about 100 yards up the hill to the right (east) of the gallows as one looks up Hangman's Gulch. The other Bannack Cemetery is located about $1^1/_2$ miles west of Bannack and dates from the mid-1870s.

7. Why can't people drive through Bannack anymore?

The managers of the state parks system decided to restrict driving through Bannack for many reasons. With increased visitation, safety and accident liability are factors. Vandalism has been reduced considerably by elimination of vehicular traffic. And, the unpaved Bannack streets get very muddy at times; eliminating driving keeps the streets in better shape and minimizes upkeep.

8. Where did Governor Sidney Edgerton live?

Governor Edgerton bought a building for $400 and had it moved to the location across from the present Visitor's Center, where the large cottonwood trees grow. The Edgerton family made the building into suitable living quarters. It eventually burned sometime in the late 1800s, after the Edgertons had moved back to Ohio. Sometime after 1900 (possibly in the 1920s), the small log house with the sod roof behind and to the right of the cottonwood trees was built from the logs of the "Governor's Mansion."

9. Is the Parks Division planning to restore any more buildings?

No, not at the present time anyway. Bannack will never be made into the rawly commercial type of attraction prevalent in many historical sites today. The aim of the Parks Division is to keep Bannack a real ghost town from the period of 1880 to 1900. Preservation ("arrested decay") is the philosophy, rather than restoration and renewal.

10. Are there rattlesnakes at Bannack?

Yes, there are, but very few are seen, and not always every year. It is always a good idea to remember the possibility of encountering rattlers, but not to hamper your tour by fearing them.

11. What are the distances to Dillon and to Virginia City?

Dillon is 25 miles from Bannack, and Virginia City is about 85 miles. (Distance from Bannack to Virginia City via the old stage road was about 70 miles).

12. What is the best way to Yellowstone National Park?

There are basically two ways depending on what you want to see.
(1). Go to Dillon and take highway 41 to Twin Bridges and then right on highway 287 to Nevada City and Virginia City and through the beautiful Madison Valley at Ennis. Continue on highway 287 by Quake Lake and Hebgen Dam, which was near the epicenter of the 1959 Madison Canyon Earthquake. From Quake Lake continue on highway 287 to West Yellowstone.
(2). Go on Interstate 15 south of Dillon to Monida on the Montana-Idaho border. Turn east at Monida on the gravel road marked Red Rock Lakes National Wildlife Refuge (this is the primary national refuge for the endangered trumpeter swan). From Lakeview continue on the gravel road to West Yellowstone. This road is gravel through the beautiful Centennial Valley from Monida nearly to

West Yellowstone, and should be attempted only in summer and dry weather. This particular route is best for seeing wildlife of all kinds, including antelope, deer, and various species of birds to include sandhill cranes and bald eagles as well as the trumpeter swan.

13. What is this strange-looking slanted structure which is seen in profusion in this part of the country?

This wooden structure is called a beaver slide or hay derrick, and is used for stacking loose hay. This type of hay stacker was invented in the Big Hole Valley, which is also called the Valley of the Ten Thousand Haystacks.

14. When did the Department of Fish, Wildlife and Parks assume management of Bannack?

In 1954 the Beaverhead County Museum donated about one third of what is now Bannack State Park to the state to preserve the site of the first capital of Montana. Through the years, the state has acquired the present 198 acres of Bannack State Park and has exclusive ownership of the entire site. The last property was acquired in 1985.

15. Was Henry Plummer the sheriff of Virginia City as well as Bannack?

Yes, Plummer was elected sheriff of Bannack on May 24, 1863 and, later that year, his jurisdiction included Alder Gulch.

16. Why was the territorial capital moved to Virginia City?

The capital of Montana Territory was moved to Virginia City (February 7, 1865) because much of the Bannack population had deserted the Grasshopper Diggings and had moved to richer placers such as Alder Gulch at Virginia City and Last Chance Gulch at Helena. The move was a matter of legislative efficiency since the center of population was nearer to Virginia City.

17. Many of the early pictures of Bannack show many more buildings than are here today. What happened to many of the buildings?

Bannack has had several major fires through the years, which took their tolls in structures and even lives—such as the 1926 fire that destroyed the F.L. Graves Store and killed F.L. Graves, Jr. Many of the buildings fell down due to deterioration. A few were moved, such as the Goodrich Hotel, which stood on the east side of Skinner's Saloon and was the first hotel in Montana. It was moved to Virginia City in the 1950s. Also, many of the buildings were torn down for their lumber or even for firewood over the years.

18. What was the peak population of Bannack?

Peak population was estimated at 3,000 people in the spring of 1863 with another 2,000 living in the surrounding hills. Population quickly dwindled with the discoveries of other nearby gold fields.
Other population figures include:
1870—255 natives, 126 foreign, 375 whites, 1 colored and 5 Chinese
1879—700 (estimate)
1880—(federal census) 232
1890—203
1900—418
1910—229
1920—59

19. What are the temperature ranges of Bannack?

Highs in the 90°F range are not uncommon in the summer, while February of 1989 recorded 62° below zero. Bannack has always been well known locally for its cold weather.

20. Are there camping facilities at Bannack?

Two campgrounds are located about one-quarter mile west of Bannack, and are administered by the Montana Department of Fish, Wildlife and Parks. The 21 camping spots each include a fireplace. There is a central lavatory facility as well as a central pump for potable water.

Left: The beaver slide haystacker was invented in the Big Hole Valley, the Land of Ten Thousand Haystacks.
Below: *Bannack's campground offers 21 spaces and such luxuries as running water (from a pump and well), a few mosquitoes, and deer who visit each morning just as the sun comes up.*

...And when the book-worm sits in shady bowers, his pleasure came through you. But, you too, live in your past. The thousands that roamed your streets are gone. The crumbling shacks that once were happy homes, will not reveal the names of those who once dwelt there. No more music stirs the busy feet in Hurdy Hall. No more the gunshot wounds the daring chief. No more, shall voices, the makers of your destiny, reverberate among your templed hills.

Professor Thomas J. Dimsdale
The Vigilantes of Montana